Whisper This . . .

Whisper This . . .
Not to Your Horse, to Yourself

A *No-Bull$#it* Book
for You and Your Horse

by Smokie Brannaman

Book design, and typesetting by Suni Hannan, Bluehorse Canyon, llc.
www.bluehorsecanyon.com

Photography by Kat Brannaman, firelite foto.
www.firelitefoto.com

Original illustrations by Travis Brannaman

Contents

Preface

When I first thought about writing a *No-Bull$#it* book about horses and their owners, I figured maybe I could help some of you out by summing things up in about 7 pages . . .

Buy

A

Good

Horse

And

Ride

It

OK, eight pages. I forgot the exclamation point **!**

It turned out to be a little more than that, but not much.

Acknowledgments

Everything that comes to pass in one's life happens for a reason. I don't know yet how this book will be interpreted, or what will become of it, or me. I'm not a famous or special person, and maybe I have no business even writing this. But my friends and family who have supported me through these troubled times and helped me get this book to print are truly the special people in this world who deserve the credit, if it's good. I'll take the blame, if it's not. To them, I offer my heartfelt thanks, and apologies, if this turns out to be *Bull$#it!*

Introduction

Now you're probably wondering just what you can learn about horsemanship or anything else horse related from someone like me. Well, someone once said, it's not always the scholar who has all to answers to the questions. Let me first tell you a little bit about me and why I'm writing this book. As I said, I am the not-so-rich-and-famous brother of one of the finest horseman and clinicians in the country, if not the world. He is, in his own right a very fine man. He has devoted his life to horses and methods of training that I will never rival, nor do I want to. I grew up with him, had the same life experiences, and the same beginning with horses. But I went into the military, made a career of it, retired, and now I'm out here in the civilian world trying to make a living and enjoying my horses just like you're trying to do. All the while trying not to go broke while continuing to learn and improve my horsemanship and that of others. I have had horses and trained my own, and other people's horses throughout my life. I've worked as a stable manager, trainer, (not what I would consider professional), and breeding farm manager as well. I've also had to opportunity to watch and talk with horseman from all over the world while doing the kings business in the military.

Does that make me an expert on horses or horsemanship? No it doesn't. It also doesn't make me a psychologist able to fix your marriage or life's problems while fixing your horses' problems at a three-day clinic.

I have done small clinics here and there for my friends, mostly for free or cold beer, just because I like to help people with their horses and I enjoy it. I've never tried to make a living at it, mostly because I have a real problem with being able to feed a line of *"Bull$#it"* to a bunch of people knowing that they will never get it, and yet still taking their hard-earned money, while believing that I am the one and only horseman in the world who can fix their horse, teach them what they need to know, or help them enjoy their horse more, just because they pay me to tell them that. Now I'm not saying that the wisdom these folks sell is not good knowledge. Today's clinicians who subscribe to natural horsemanship, the vaquero methods or any of the other topics you care to mention are all very useful to you and me. I use a lot of it in working with horses as well, and I have learned something from all of them. I'll repeat that, *all of them.* (More on that topic later) So, now that you know that I'm just a guy who might be able to give you some insight on enjoying your horse experience a little more and give you some straight talking *"No-Bull$#it"* advise without paying a ton of money, read on.

Or, put this back on the shelf and continue to believe you'll be the next horse whisperer by doing a clinic once a year, spending a bunch of money, and thinking "All that and I'll only have to ride that horse once a week."

A note from the Author...

I would like to thank all the folks who have purchased a copy of my book, *Whisper This* and I hope that it will help you in your quest to become better educated about the equine world and the horses we enjoy. Your purchase is helping to make the Horseman's Services Scholarship Project become a reality!

For more information on the project go to:
www.smokiebrannaman.com

I have read with great interest the comments sent to me about the content of this book. I do appreciate the opinions of others, be they good or bad. I even want to know about what they think is just Bull$#it!.

SO, I have added this page in hopes of setting a couple of things straight before you start reading. It has been mentioned by a number of people that I should have explained some of the terms such as *"green broke"*, *"cribbing"* and *"criped orchid"* *etc*. That way the readers would better understand what I was saying. Well, here's my answer to that:

You need to look it up BEFORE you buy a "cryptorchid horse"! (I spelled it wrong in the book...sorry!)

Now that we got that out of the way, enjoy the book!

Whisper This . . .

Chapter One

Why Do You Want a Horse?

This is the first question you must ask yourself. Why do I want a 1200-pound animal that could potentially bite me, kick me, stomp on my feet, or buck me off? If your answer is "Well I saw this movie" or "I had horses when I was young and..." you better take a step back and reevaluate your reasons for becoming a horse owner. First off, I would put most people into two categories when it comes to having horses. Or even other pets or animals for that matter. These categories are, Horse Lovers and Horsemen. Sure you could say, well I might not be the man from Snowy River but I can ride pretty well so I'm kind of a horseman. Or, I love my horses so what's wrong with that? My horse is my best friend yada, yada. Well there's nothing wrong with that. But if your entire reason for getting a horse is because you have watched a movie, read a book, took a couple of classes, just love horses or what ever, and now you think I'll just run out and buy a horse.... I'll wait to read the article:

Local Horse Owner Learns There Are More Ways to Earn Frequent Flyer Miles!

If your sole reason for getting a horse is based on some fantasy about Black Beauty, The Horse Whisperer, or becoming the next rich and famous horse trainer, your going to be in for a very rude awakening. Owning and riding horses, or training horses, is a commitment that has a lot more to it than just going out and buying one. Things to consider are boarding costs, vet bills, farrier bills, feed, etc. If you're lucky enough to have your own place to keep a horse, there's fence building, hauling hay, cleaning stalls and taking care of those horses. 24 hours a day, 365 days a year. And that's just to say, I have a horse. Most people don't have the time to spend with their kids, let alone a horse, every single day. But, if your determined to get one, have given serious thought to what it will take in terms of your commitment to yourself and your horse then I'll try to help.

First off, all fantasies aside, what do you really want to do with your horse? This is the most important question you have to answer. Do you want to just ride trails, work cows, do horse shows, or race him?

You need to be honest with yourself and realize that the pretty little filly with the four white socks is probably just pretty. It will not be a trail-broke, well-trained horse that you can trust to put your kids on.

Most people who show up at clinics with problems are not there because they necessarily have a problem horse. They are there because they made a wrong choice in buying that horse in the first place. Or, they overestimated their abilities and underestimate the time it takes to deal with a particular horse. But . . .

Some very knowledgeable horsemen will stand up and tell you, There's no such thing as a bad horse just bad owners... Well I'm here to tell ya folks, that's just plain Bull$#it! And if you use a little common sense you'll understand why.

I worked as manager and trainer of young horses on a breeding farm in Wisconsin. This farm has 40 to 50 broodmares, 10 breeding stallions and over 100 young horses. These horses are Russian Akhaltekes and Friesians.

At any given time I had 10 to 15 colts I worked with on a daily basis; feeding, doctoring, halter breaking, and starting under saddle. I also had anywhere from 10 to 20 new colts born every year.

Now, think about this… If I had 20 new colts every year, what are the odds that every single one of them is going to be good horse? Have these all-knowing horseman forgotten about birth defects and that horses can have them as well as humans? What kind of a horse would you have if at birth, that colt were deprived of oxygen just long enough to destroy a part of his brain that allows him to think and move like a normal horse would? Every reputable horse breeder in the country breeds horses for a specific job, ability, temperament, color, or a combination of all or some of these qualities. The good ones are kept. The bad ones that don't meet the standards are culled out, sold as grades, or destroyed. Here's another question. If I bred an Akhalteke, (A horse that was originally bred as a cavalry horse for the Russian Army) to say, a pony, am I going to get a gentle horse I can put my mother on? Probably not. All I'll get is a bigger pony that's meaner and tougher. This does not necessarily make him a bad horse for someone who wants a horse like that, but he's still a bad horse for you. There's a saying out there that goes. *If you breed a dingbat mare, to a dingbat stud, you'll most likely get a DINGBAT COLT.* That's right folks, not a good horse. Let's take this a step further. When I first took the job at the breeding farm, I walked into a barn filled with 42 yearlings and two-year olds. When I opened the first stall, all I saw was a brown blur as it ran over the top of me on its way out the barn. Was this a bad colt? Well at the time it was. But over the next three months this colt was worked with, handled every day, and eventually turned into a pretty nice horse. On the other hand, there was "Peron", another colt the same age. This colt had the same care and treatment as the other colts in the barn but this one was different. In the first week he reared up and struck me with both front feet, stomped me when he got me down and went through or jumped the round pen fence twice, dragging me down the road with him. Was he a good horse? Not hardly. I sent him out to get gelded hoping that might settle him down some but it didn't. He was still just as wild and aggressive as he always was. He is now filling a better position in the food chain *BECAUSE HE WAS NOT A GOOD HORSE!!!!* I can't say what made him that way or if he could have been turned around given enough time, but... some better trainers then me wouldn't touch him and that tells me he just might be one of those unheard of bad horses.

There is more to think about when it comes to buying a horse than just picking out the pretty one or the breed that sounds cool. You need to pick out the horse that will work for you. One that will cause the least amount of difficulty, expense in training, or retraining, and has the personality and breeding that fits your riding ability and type of riding you want to do. That doesn't mean you can't get a pretty one too, but it is not the first consideration.

There are lots of good horses out there, so why buy an idiot and think you'll be able to have a good time fixing all his problems?

Buying a racehorse off the track to use as a kids trail horse doesn't make a whole lot of sense to me but people do it all the time. Why? Because he's pretty or he'll be put down if you don't save him. That's not a good reason. Why do you think he's for sale in the first place? Because he's not good for what the owner wants to do with him, that's why. He can't run (fast enough) but he's too fast to be a trail horse. He's crippled (that lets out cowpony) and so on. Horses are bred for a purpose. Race horses, cow horses, driving horses, etc.

Can they be something else? Sure they can. But do you have the time and experience to train him to do it? I'm betting not. So why not get a good horse that's bred and trained for what you want to do and enjoy him rather that getting a mustang and trying to make him into a kids horse? It'll be a whole lot healthier, I'll tell you that. As a general rule, you have hot-blooded horses, warm bloods, cold bloods and draft horses. All were bred for a specific purpose in mind. Hot-blooded horses like Akhaltekes were bred to be war-horses. They are tough, fast and extremely intelligent. In fact they are some of the most intelligent horses I have ever worked with. But... with a few exceptions they are not a horse for a beginner. They do not take kindly to being handled hard when training them, and if you piss one off, you had better bring a lunch and be prepared to go the distance because they will be. Not what I would consider a horse for a leisurely ride down the trail or a western pleasure prospect. I have mostly had quarter horses and I think they are probably the best all around horse you can have. But I bought an Akhalteke too. Why? Because my hobby is Civil War reenacting in the First Alabama Cavalry. Pagnio's blood-lines are from horses that were bred to be cavalry horses. He is loyal, fearless, tough, and intelligent. And he is also gentle and easy going as far as Akhaltekes go. Plus, I know how to train him and ride him for what he was meant for. That is the difference between me and someone else who buys a horse because he's just cool or good-looking. Incidentally, Pagnio is both cool and pretty good-looking too! Blood bay with four white socks.

If you are going out to buy a horse, be honest with yourself. If you don't know what to look for, find someone you trust to help find the right horse. In most cases, you can't make a reining horse out of a Belgian, a western pleasure horse from Sea Biscuit, or a pulling horse from a POA. That's Pony of America... not "Piece of A$$" for you computer text-message types. You will learn as you continue reading that you can have a lot more fun with the right horse and spend a lot less money in the process.

Chapter Two

Now I'm Ready to Find a Good Horse

OK! Now we've established some ground rules on getting your horse. And, if you're being honest with yourself, you know what you want a horse for, what kind of a horse you need to look for, and what it's going to take to keep this horse and do the right thing for you and him. Now you need to know where you can find this horse, and what will it cost? Lets take this in two different parts. First, the horse. You need to find a horse that fits the exact needs of you or anyone else who will be riding him. If you need a good, well-broke horse that you or your kids will be safe on, then that's what you need to look for.

THAT WILL NOT BE A GREEN-BROKE THREE YEAR OLD THAT IS GENTLE WITH LOTS OF POTENTIAL! $250.00 OBO!

What you will be looking for is an older, well-broke horse that has been used for the type of riding your interested in doing. Older means 8-years old or more. Horses do not mature mentally until they are between 8 and 10-years old. Anything less than that and you are looking at a continual training process until they get that old. If you fancy yourself as an up and coming horse trainer, by all means, go out and get that colt or green-broke horse and go to town. Once you've healed up, come back and read on. Then I'll try to show you the mistake you made and help you with that young horse when you're ready. Start your search with the local farriers in your area. They will know just about every horse their customers have for sale and then some. They will be able to tell you what bad habits they might have if they are a client horse and what kind of shape the horse is in. Another good source is your local horse vet. They see horses all over the country and can give you a wealth of information on horses that they know of. Generally, vets don't recommend horses to buy that are bad tempered that they might have to work on. If there are good trainers in your area, you can ask them for advise on horses for sale. However, if they have horses for sale as well, take that into account. Horse-trading is like used cars; everyone has the one that was only rode to church by a little old lady. Horse sales can be a good thing or a very bad thing. Most sales take horses on consignment and they know very little about what the horse is like or where it came from other than what the seller is willing to divulge.

I have bought horses thru the ring that have been outstanding horses. But, I kinda know what I'm looking for. I'm betting you don't or you wouldn't be reading this book. Private horse sales from reputable breeders can be a very good way to get the horse your looking for but you still need to make sure it's the right horse for you. Today's popular horse seems to be "the ranch-broke horse". It is all the rage. Pay big bucks and you'll have the horse of your dreams. Ranch-broke horses are very good and you will have a horse that can be the horse of your dreams if you pay 10 or 20 thousand dollars. *The only difference between a ranch-broke horse and a horse that has been rode a lot is where it came from and the price.*

I was at a horse sale not long ago and a green-broke 4-year old, registered quarter horse gelding came thru the ring. The man riding him raised and trained him. He was selling him because he just had too many horses. This gelding walked into the ring surrounded by about 100 people like he'd done it all his life. He walked, trotted, cantered, stopped, and backed up like a champ. His rider pulled down a rope swung it around, dropped it down, put it on a foot and picked it up, wrapped it around his feet then unwrapped it with no fuse no muss. That horse sold for $800.00 and I sure wish I had bought him.

But, I was helping another person find a good horse. If he had gone through a ranch-broke horse sale he would have gone for many times that. I'm not saying that you can get the horse of your dreams for $800 but they are out there. All you have to do is look. The bottom line is this—it's not what you have to pay, it's what you get for the money!

And I'll tell you this . . . A FREE HORSE IS NOT FREE!!!!! I don't care who tells you what. If it's free, there is a catch and you or someone else will pay for it.

Sometimes in the horse world the saying still holds true— you get what you pay for. But, I'll bet the $40,000.00 bridle horse you buy won't stand rock solid still when you shoot a 54 caliber sharps carbine off its back like my $2000.00 cavalry horse will. And, she's gentle enough to put my kids and their friends on too. It all boils down to what you want in a horse, what your willing to spend, and how much work you want to put into it. If you don't get a good horse to start with, you're only in for a world of problems and not going to enjoy having the horse or what you're doing. Last but not least, don't let someone tell you that there's only one breed that will work for what you want. "Oh, you've got to have a quarter horse or a saddle bred" etc, etc. There are good horses in every breed and bad horses in every breed and not a single one is the best at everything. Every horseman or trainer is particular about the horses he prefers for whatever reason but that should not be your reason for getting a particular breed of horse. Many grade horses have made just as good a trail horse or cow pony as the top blood lines in the country. Unless you are breeding for money or showing, papers don't mean much on a horse, especially on a gelding. It will give you an idea of what that horse might be capable of doing or being but…. If you're buying a good gentle horse to ride down the trail, why do you care if his granddad was a grand champion halter horse? And lets not forget soundness and physical condition. Price is not an indication of how good the horse is, or if it is physically fit, or has the confirmation to perform the job you bought him for.

I know of a person who bought an exotic breed stallion for breeding (without a vet check) and paid $50,000.00. Less than two months later he had the horse at a university medical vet school getting him gelded because he was criped orchid and had mutant sperm. Now he has a very expensive riding horse.

Young horses that appear to be very well trained and ready to go should be checked with great care. If they are that far along in their training at two or three years old they could be candidates for early leg problems, arthritis or other soundness issues. Bones and joints on young horses are not usually mature until they are four years old. That does not mean you can't ride them before that but you must take it easy and not overwork them. Many trainers need to get horses to the show ring and win as soon as they can in order to make money. What happens after that is someone else's problem and that just might be you if your not careful.

Older horses can have issues as well. Some will show signs of arthritis, founder or other issues that can be masked with drugs by an unscrupulous seller. And even the wildest horse can be as gentle as a lamb with enough rompin or ace in him. If you have any doubt about a horse, have a vet check him out or come back unannounced in a day or two and see if it is still the same horse you looked at the other day.

I've seen people buy a horse without even riding him. What the hell is up with that? Do you go to a car dealership and fork out 20 grand for a new truck after watching the salesman drive it around the block?

Then why would you buy a horse based only on how the seller can ride him or tells you how he rides or how well broke he is? If your not comfortable getting on a strange horse, then you might be out of your league in dealing with that horse when you get him home. I would suggest taking a knowledgeable horseman along on your horse hunting trips. Rely on him to point out the finer details to look for when evaluating a potential candidate. Let him take that first ride before you get on to see if this horse might work for you. But sooner or later, you better get on too! Lets move on to some of the things I look for in a horse I'd consider buying.

Chapter Three

What to Look For in a Good Horse

What I look for in a horse when I'm in the market to buy one can be used to evaluate just about any animal, but I will deal with horses. After all, this book isn't about buying or training cats! (Those little eatin, crappin, furballs that . . .) I'd better get back to the subject here. When I look at a horse to buy, after having an idea of what kind of horse I'm looking for, (i.e. older kids horse, colt, etc.) I have seven specific things I look at in this order:

1. Personality
2. Brains
3. Confirmation
4. Deformities or physical problems
5. Feet
6. Training or the lack there of
7. Eye appeal

You will notice that eye appeal is the last thing I look at. Now I'll be honest and tell you that I will tend to pick out the pretty ones first as well. But that's only because a butt ugly horse will not re-sell no matter how good they are. That's just a fact of life and to a certain extent has to be taken into account if you plan on selling him sometime down the road. Lets take each one of these items individually and I'll try to explain in more detail.

Personality: When I start to evaluate a horse's personality, I start by watching how he acts in the pasture around other horses, or by himself, or in his stall. I would prefer that I could observe him without him knowing I'm there. Why you ask? Because I'm not going to be in that pasture or barn every minute and I want to know what he'll be like when the boss is not around. Does he get along with other horses or tend to fight? That's important to know if you're planning on riding with your friends or he needs to fit in with the heard. Does he try to push down the fences to eat on the other side? Does he crib? Cribbing is a habit that will not stop and can kill him in certain cases. I wouldn't buy a cribber or wind sucker if it were the last horse on earth. If there are distractions around the field, such as cars going by, farm equipment, load noises, etc, observe how he reacts to this. Does he run clear across the pasture if a car goes by? If he's in a stall, does he pace back and forth or stand quietly and munch hay? Again, watch and look for signs of cribbing. I am not an advocate of stalling horses because I believe that it will only eventually lead to personality problems and bad habits. But I guess they all can't be outside in today's urban horse world. I will tell you that nine times out of ten a horse that stays outside will be more easy going, trainable, relaxed, and healthier than one that is locked up all the time and not allowed interaction with other horses. Once I'm satisfied that this horse or horses are worthy of more than a casual look, I'll move on to part two of my personality evaluation. What I want to look for now is how he reacts to people.

When I walk into the pasture, does he pick up his head and look? What is his next reaction? Does he turn and face me, start to come in my direction, or look for the closest escape route? At first I will make no attempt to walk directly toward him or any other horse in the pasture. I want to know if he is comfortable with humans in his space or thinks you're the enemy. Ideally, the horse that will draw my attention is the one that willingly comes over for a closer look. If he does come over the things I look for are, jerking his head up if I try to pet his forehead, or swishing his tail if I try to pet his hip or walk behind him. These are signs of agitation or aggression that could mean his first reaction is a kick if something scares him or he doesn't like what I'm doing. LOOK AT THE EYES!!! Are they rolled back in his head, white around the corners, or wild looking? Or are they soft, intelligent, and inquisitive? How are his manners? Does he try to walk over the top of you, or to take a bite out of your arm? Can you rub him all over including his legs and ears? Will he follow you if you walk a few steps away? Is he still respectful if another horse comes up? If the answer is not positive to one or more of these questions, especially his eyes and raising your hand to pet his head or swishing the tail, WALK AWAY AND BUY A HORSE ANOTHER DAY!

You may have noticed that I have made no mention yet of putting on a halter or trying to catch him. That's because you will pretty much know if you can catch him if he comes up. I want to know that this horse will be a willing and trusting partner without having to tie him to a tree just to pet him. Now is the time to get out my genuine (Insert clinician name here) rope halter and lead and take a much closer look at this prospective horse.

Brains: After the initial first look and observing his personality, I'll have a pretty good idea what kind of mind this horse has. Now what I want to look for is how he responds to pressure. That doesn't mean I'm going to lay into him, start jacking on the halter, or see just how far I can push this horse to get a reaction. First and foremost if you are buying any horse, except a weanling, they should be halter broke. If they're not, you have a problem and for the most part it's going to go down hill from there. I will ask the seller what kind of work he's done with the young horse or the older broke horse then see what he really knows or is capable of understanding. Mind you I am not moving into a training evaluation, just some basic stuff. Will he lead out willingly without balking? Will he move away when I turn into him or can I encourage it with minimal resistance? Will he back up? Will he give to the lead without getting upset? Can I do this from both sides of his body?

If you haven't been told this, there is something that you really need to know about how a horse thinks… The two hemispheres of a horses' brain do not work together. They don't think the same way with both sides and they are not connected to communicate back and forth.

Lets explore this a little more.

What that means in terms of training and handling horses is that what a horse reacts to on one side does not mean he'll do the same thing on the other side. Most horses are more comfortable with people being on their left side. That's because that's where most people spend the most time. Saddling, leading, getting on, etc. are all done on the left so a horse get use to you being there. Why don't you try taking your dead broke horse out someday and try to saddle him from the right? Did he think nothing of it or was he a little skittish? I think you'll begin to understand what I mean. Or think about this. Have you ever been out on a trail ride and gone by something that you thought your horse was going to absolutely blow a gasket at when he saw it? Then, as you got closer he just walked on by like there was nothing to be upset about and he was wondering why you were tense. But on the way back you go by the same booger bait, you're not paying attention and the next thing you know you're looking up at the sky and your horse is blowing snot far enough to bring you out of your haze when it hits your face! This happened because he was looking and reacting to what he saw with the other side of his brain. In effect, that object was totally new and not seen before by your horse!

One of the most important things that I try to teach people is to remember to do everything from both sides of your horse. Groundwork, saddling, getting on, flagging, everything.

Back to the evaluation.

By doing these basic things in terms of handling, yielding to pressure, and working on both sides I'll be able to get a reasonably good idea of this horses intelligence. If he crowds me too close when I lead him, and I give him a bump to move him off, does he learn it quickly and remember? Can I encourage him to move in a circle around me without getting upset? If you are satisfied that he can think and respond, then let's move on to confirmation.

Confirmation: Confirmation is the basic physical structure of a horse that will determine whether or not he is going to be suitable for the type of riding you will be doing. Every horse will have some imperfection in his or her confirmation, but in reality you need to determine if that is going to prevent him from doing the job. There are numerous good books out there that can explain it a lot better than I can in the space of a paragraph or two so I'll just hit the high points. The biggies are straight legs, good back, bone structure, and muscle. If a horse has crooked legs, he's not going to move naturally or be handy in terms of performance. That is not as much of a problem for a horse used to just walk down the trail, but would not work for a cutting horse. Bad backs are probably the hardest things to understand. If you have a horse with a long back, he might be real smooth to ride but if you put him into a situation where he needs to get up under himself to turn fast and he might pile you and him up.

The same goes for bone structure and muscle. If a horse is frail boned and has weak muscles and you try to make a jumper or endurance horse out of him, you'll most likely end up with a crippled horse. Every riding discipline has a different idea of the ideal confirmation and I cannot possibly go into them all. But in my opinion for general riding your looking for a horse with sound straight legs, a medium to short back with strong bones, and well-defined muscles, especially over the hip and chest. In short, if a horse looks extremely long and frail, or the parts just don't look good together, then maybe you should take a pass or get an expert opinion.

Deformities: This kind of goes hand in hand with confirmation, but there are some things that I look for that wouldn't necessarily, but could detract from the horses ability. What I'm looking at is any scars, indications of injury like shin splints, wind puffs, a thick neck from founder, or birth defects, etc. I have a mare that can't pee straight. When she goes, it runs down the side of her leg and makes a constant stain that I have to clean and occasionally doctor when it gets raw. This doesn't affect her performance or soundness but it looks bad and would probably not make her a good halter horse candidate.

Feet: It could probably be argued that feet should be higher up on the list and in some cases I would agree. Without a good foot all you have is a horse statue that you have to clean up after and feed. It probably would be cheaper to buy one of those concrete ones! It would be best to have a good farrier whom you trust do this for you, but suffice it to say if you look at a horse and his feet are not trimmed, are broken, cracked, or just don't look right, you need to look closer. Lameness issues can sometimes be detected as well. Ringbone, navicular, and founder are all serious concerns that will affect the soundness of your horse, now or in the future.

Training: (Or the lack there of) You have already established what you are looking for in terms of how well a horse must be trained in order to meet your needs. So now is the time for the test drive. What I try to do is get the seller to ride him first. This way I can watch how the horse moves, see what kind of response he gets from different ques, etc. This will also allow you to judge just how confident the seller is about getting on this well-broke horse. If he offers up some excuse about being hurt at work or something, chances are he got hurt on that horse. At least that's how I would interpret it. If he's selling this horse as a kids horse, ask if he has any kids and would they ride it? If the answer is no, then find another horse. If things are looking good up to now, it's time for you (or your trusted friend first) to step up to the plate and get on. Your first ride should be in an area that you are comfortable in, like an arena or round pen so if things go wrong, help can get there quicker. But remember, if your buying a trail horse or a cow horse for team penning, you won't know if he is one unless you go out on the trail or chase down a cow. If it is possible to get this horse out and see what he'll do in the woods, then by all means do it.

It's better to find out before you buy him that he won't cross the creek rather then when the bear is on your ass and he wont go!

I won't go into what to look for when buying a young horse that needs some training, because I don't think most people who read this book are ready at this point to do it. But I will address this in more depth in another chapter. If we're still good to go at this point, lets look at the last topic.

Eye appeal: My basic answer to anyone asking about which horse to buy when the topic of pretty comes up is "You can't ride pretty". Now as I said earlier, it is dang hard to sell a butt ugly horse. However, good horses will sell. If given a choice between and very pretty horse that I think might be a little hardheaded and a not so pretty horse with a lot of brains and ability, then I'll take the not so pretty one. Nuff said.

I once had a horse on the ranch when I was a kid that was a leopard appaloosa gelding named Tank. And let me tell ya folks, this horse was pretty damn ugly! Over sixteen hands tall, a head about as log as your arm, roman nosed and all them spots! I wouldn't be caught dead on that horse at a rodeo or in public unless there was a whole lot of money involved. But I rode that horse on the forest permits checking cows, doctoring, dragging bulls out of the bog, and moving hot tired brushed up herds out to other pastures, and I'll tell you what... Tank was the best damn brush bustin, cow pulling, roping, sure-footed mountain horse we had for that job! And if it wasn't for him, I might still be up there trying to get that damn bull out of the bog! He was a good horse where pretty just didn't matter!

Chapter Four

You Might Be Ready to Buy if . . .

Can I buy one now??? Can I? Can I? Well, yes you can, but I wouldn't recommend it just yet. I'm going to assume that everything has gone as planned up to this point. But there are a few things that I would highly recommend to you before you plunk down that check. This is reality speaking here.

I know damn good and well that by now most of you have reverted back to your Disneyland mentality and have absolutely fallen in love with this perfect horse and you just have to have him no matter what. Am I right?

You know I am, if you're being honest with yourself. So step back, take a breath, and come back to my *No Bull$#it* world.

YOU NEED TO GET A VET CHECK AND HAVE YOUR FARRIER LOOK AT HIM IF YOUR NOT SURE ABOUT HIS FEET!

Getting a vet check will be an additional cost to you up front, but it just might save you thousands of dollars down the road. We, and I mean me too, are not the all-knowing experts on horse problems, disease, soundness, or a number of other things that a vet can check out. I look at it as just like buying a used car. You don't buy a used car without having your mechanic look at it first do you? Well maybe you do. But unlike buying a horse, I know that most of you will just sell the lemon and get another one when it comes to a car. But you won't sell that problem horse if he is a lemon, will you? You will just keep dumping more money into it hoping things will work out until you're broke or he dies. Sorry folks, that's just the cold hard facts of what I have seen out there in the horse world. PLEASE get a vet check.

The last thing I'd like to recommend is to take a day or two to think this over. You are about to make a big commitment in time and money that you may regret for the next 20 years. Go back and take another look at the other horse that might have worked out if you hadn't found Black Beauty. Come back and take him for another ride and do a little more with him. Then if you're sure this is the one, get that horse of your dreams. Then read on and see that your adventure is just beginning!

Chapter Five

Now the Work Starts
and Reality Sets In

As I've said through out this book, there is more to owning a horse than just going out and buying one. Now you have to provide for, take care of, and give this horse a job to do. After all, you didn't buy him as a pasture ornament, did you? If you did, you might as well sell him to someone else right now and buy a stuffed animal to put on your mantle or a picture to put in your wallet, because this is where most people start to have problems.

The first problem you're going to encounter is finding the time to spend with your new toy. Oh sure, you'll be out there every day brushing and petting and riding a little for the first week or so until the honeymoon is over and the novelty wears off. Then it will go to maybe every other day or maybe once or twice a week. Before you know it, you'll be out on the weekends or you'll wave to him in the pasture once in while as you go to work. Don't think it will happen to you? Well, I hope for the horse's sake it doesn't. But I've seen it at just about every stable, barn, or farm I've been to. So, odds are it will happen, if you don't do something about it. I'm not trying to discourage you right off the bat, but my whole purpose in writing this is to try to prevent some of the things I see wrong out there in the horse world. Time and time again I've seen good horses turn into brombies with bad manners and habits, or neglected to the point of almost what I would consider abuse because the owners just didn't have the time.

I don't know how many times I've gone to a clinic or had someone talk to me about the problems they're having with their horses, and the most consistent thing I hear is, *Geez, I don't know what happened. He wasn't like that when I bought him.* Take a minute and try to answer that question before I tell you why that is. Give up? Here's the reason:

BECAUSE YOU HAVEN'T RIDIN HIM ENOUGH!

It shouldn't take a rocket scientist to figure out that a horse will forget how to be a good horse if he's not reminded regularly. Good ranch broke horses are that way and sell for big bucks because they were rode *a lot* and often. They have a job to do on a regular basis. That doesn't mean once a week, or once a month, it's about every day. You and I both know that unless you're retired or rich that is not possible to do. But you have to make the commitment to give your horse something to do on a regular basis or he'll figure out something on his own. An older well-broke horse doesn't need riding every day to stay in shape or remain a well-broke horse. But once a month won't work either. I'd ride at least twice a week if I could and three would be better. But if all you can do is ride on a weekend, why not see if there is someone else who can ride him some?

There are people out there who will exercise your horse for a nominal fee. Or find someone who knows how to ride who can't afford his or her own horse. They would probably love to get some saddle time and maybe pay you to do it! Just make sure that whomever you let ride knows what they're doing and won't ruin your horse or get them hurt.

If you just can't ride as much as you would like, at least do something on a regular basis that will keep him thinking. Learn how to do some groundwork with him. Get him better on the halter, or softer in the face and able to move his feet better. Do some flagging, or work with desensitizing him with plastic bags, walking over tarps or that maybe that rain slicker you might need to put on some day. There are a lot of good books and videos at your local library that you can borrow *free* to learn more. (Providing you are willing to put the time into him) If not, refer back to the part about selling him and buying a picture!

If you went out on a limb against my recommendation and bought a young horse, you had better find a way to ride three or four times a week or you're going to be in serious trouble.

If you don't give him a job to do regularly, the famous quotes you hear about riding by "Feel" will mean... feel your ass hitting the ground regularly!

Chapter Six

Care and Feeding

This is a chapter that can be very controversial. I'm going to try to give you some straight common sense explanations of why I think today's feeding and nutrition programs are just a crock. For thousands of years, horses lived wild and evolved all over the world. We, as the dominant and more mentally advanced species, (that could be debatable), came along and domesticated them for our needs. Before that they pretty much survived just fine on their own without a nutrition expert figuring out how they're suppose to eat and what kind of food they need to survive. Today we have as many choices in horse feed, grain, vitamins, supplements, and various concoctions as we do in your local grocery store. All are designed to make your horse bigger, stronger, faster, shinier etc, etc, etc. And it all costs a lot of money.

Someone once ask me why I wouldn't take money for helping her with her horse. What I told her was, "If I take your money, then I feel that I'll have to tell you what you want to hear. But, if you're not paying me to give you all the answers you want to hear, and you ask me if I think your horse is too fat, I'm going to tell you your horse is too fat! And I don't care whether you like it or not. And by the way, you could give your horse a brake and drop a few pounds yourself." (I didn't say that last line, but maybe someone should do that for some of us once in while).

So with that in mind, this is what I think of how people feed horses today. *TOO FRIKEN MUCH!* Most horses, (with the real working horses being the exception), are being fed hay, grain, various supplements for a shinier coat, or better feet, various vitamins and maybe out on pasture on top of that. They just don't need all that crap. Why? Think about this. If you go out west and look at a heard of wild horses in Nevada, do you find a bunch of scrubby horses happily munching away on an Omalene pasture? Then maybe trot over to sweet feed patch for desert? Oh, and don't forget they're drinking from that vitamin fortified pond too! No. What you'll see for the most part is tough, lean, horses with shiny coats and hard feet. And what is their nutrition program?—grass, water, and a salt lick! I challenge you to go into any boarding stable barn in the country and what you will find is quality hay, a grain bin full of sweet feed, a shelf full of every owner's different supplements, *and a barn full of horses that are too fat and wired for sound!* Grain, and sweet feed in particular, is a carbohydrate (sugar) not protein or fat. It is used for extra energy fast in horses that work a lot, not for putting on weight or to make up for bad hay. Yes, your horse will gain weight on it too, but not good weight, just fat in all the wrong places, just like humans. And it also makes him hotter and more energetic. That might be fine if your doing a 12-hour ride on your working cow horse to gather cattle off the mountain. But it won't be so good if your planning an hour ride with your kids after you've let him stand in the stall all week and pounded ten pounds of sweet feed into him a day.

Take a look at the pictures in this chapter. They show a number of different horses all on different feeding programs. Can you tell which ones are mine and which ones get supplements, and grain in addition to hay? I'll bet you can't.

All photos are courtesy of Firelite Foto, my enterprising daughter Kat Brannaman. My artistic son, Travis Brannaman, drew all illustrations. I need to give credit where credit is due! And I think they've done a pretty good job, too!

(1)
8-YEAR-OLD MARE

(2)
14-YEAR-OLD MARE

(3)
6-YEAR-OLD MARE

(4)
10-YEAR-OLD MARE

(5)
12-YEAR-OLD GELDING

(6)
11-YEAR-OLD GELDING

(7)
2-YEAR-OLD GELDING

(8)
4-YEAR-OLD GELDING

(9)
6-YEAR-OLD MARE

(10)
12-YEAR-OLD STALLION

Ok, you looked at these pictures. Can you tell me which ones are just eating grass or hay and which ones get grain and or supplements? If you can, maybe you have a potential career as a horse nutritionist! But I'm betting you can see very little difference, if any, in how these horses look. They are all in good or too good of a shape (fat). They have shiny coats and healthy looks to them. Do you want to know who is who? Ok I'll tell you.

Pictures 1,6,7,and 9 are my horses. They were taken this summer around the pasture here at the house. All they had done to them before the pictures was brush off the mud! My horses are on grass pasture during the summer supplemented with good quality hay, if the grass gets thin. They have all the fresh water they can drink and a salt/mineral block in the trough. That's it, no more no less. In the winter it's the same thing, just substitute hay for grass. With one exception, I will give them a cup or two of grain in the morning if it's been stormy or really cold all night. And all that does is give them a little jump-start on their boilers!

Pictures 2,3,4,and 5, were taken at a local boarding stable. These horses are the typical horses you would expect to see. All of them get hay, grain, and some are on one or more supplements in addition to some pasture time. Some are too fat, like the horse in picture number 3, and the horse in picture 2 could lose some to help out that bad back. And some look pretty good, all things being considered.

Pictures 8 and 10 were taken at a breeding farm and show barn. The four-year old is getting ten pounds of fortified sweet feed a day plus various supplements for a shiny coat, better feet, etc. The stallion is a show horse and gets just about everything you can imagine! But does he really look that much better than the grass fed horses?

Supplements: I am by all means not a nutritional expert any more than I am the all-knowing horseman. But common sense should tell most folks that too much of a good thing is still a bad thing. And that's kinda how I feel about supplements. First of all, horses' bodies are designed to extract the needed vitamins and minerals from the food sources God made for them to eat. *GRASS! Not molasses, corn, and oats all balled up with riboflavin, zinc, platinum, B106, our own special sauce, and MSG to preserve the flavor!* If the quality of your pastures or hay is good, they will get all they need to survive.

If you start adding a bunch of crap to their diet, after a while their system will quit making their own and shut down. Or in the case of minerals such as selenium, they overdose and die.

Not a good thought is it. The supplement industry is just like the diet pill industry… if it really worked as good as they say, why is there another one just around the corner to try? And the same company makes it!! What happened? Wasn't the first one that you sold me supposed to cure everything… or was it really not so good after all?

No, it was probably just what they said it was. But in order to make more money they gotta get that new and improved formula out there so you'll just have to try it! Horses and people can benefit from certain supplements in their diet that will make them healthier or correct some deficiency, but don't go out and buy all this crap and start feeding it to your horse without first checking with your vet or getting an expert opinion on what he might or might not need.

Here's another tidbit for you.

If you like a horse that bites, go ahead and keep hand feeding him all those wonderful little horse cookies! In the case of an Akhalteke or a stud colt that likes to bite in the first place, he won't just nip your fingers; he'll chew your arm off at the shoulder!

Put your horse treats in a bucket or in the trough (if you just have to spend more money on sugar treats) and quit teaching your horse another bad habit!

If your horse is under weight then by all means feed him more. But that should be more hay and maybe some extra fat, not extra sugar or a lot of supplements! There are various minerals that may be lacking in your horses diet due to the soil content in your part of the country. Selenium is low up here in Wisconsin so that is one I'll mix on the hay regularly or maybe in a little grain as a treat. Check with your Ag. agent. He will be able to tell you what might be short and also check the quality of your hay or pastures. If your doing any more than that and your horse still looks bad, then you have something more serious to deal with and you had better find some expert help.

Any questions? Good!

Now get that candy bar out of your mouth and go take your horse for a ride! You and he will look and feel better for it!

Chapter Seven

Farrier Care, the Vet, and Shots

This is the only thing I'm going to say about that.

If you don't get your horses vaccinated and wormed regularly, your stupid, and somebody should slap you up side your head!

Horses don't stop getting sick just because they're not around other sick horses, and mosquitoes still fly, as far as I know. Get them done or get another hobby. Don't forget about his teeth either. (Maybe that's why he's under weight) Your vet can tell you more. You also need to get a good farrier and have his feet taken care of regularly. Keeping your horses' feet in good shape is just as important as keeping good tires on your car. You won't go very far if they're bad.

Ok, I'm going to say something more about vet care and the costs, and you are not going to like what I have to say. But if I don't tell you, I don't know of many other people who will. You won't find it in "my little pony" or horse sense for dummies either. If you have horses long enough, sooner or later, something will happen that will be really serious and will potentially cost you many hundreds or thousands of dollars in vet bills and still not guarantee that your horse will be ok when it's all said and done. So now you are faced with the hard choice of letting him go, or trying everything under the sun to save him no matter what the cost, or not thinking about what the quality of his life will be if he makes it and is not completely cured.

Folks, this is the real world out here, and every living thing in it gets old, or crippled, has an injury that cannot be fixed, and dies. Think about the horse first and do everything you can within reason. But, don't spend your life savings trying to save an animal or prolong that old foundered horse's life simply because you are still living life in some movie fantasy. Put him down. He'll understand and thank you for it.

Chapter Eight

Your Gear

I probably could have put this chapter somewhere up near the top cuz you won't be riding much if you don't have a saddle and all the goodies that go along with it. But, getting the right equipment is not a subject that should take up a lot of space. In one sentence I can tell you what you need to know.... *Get the very best saddle and equipment you can afford.* That about sums it up. But let me go a bit farther and tell you a few things.

I have a genuine handmade Wade saddle, built by a very good saddle maker, just like (Insert famous trainer name here) rides. If you wanted to buy one, it would probably go for about five grand, maybe more. Made from top quality material, rawhide tree, Monel stirrups, just like all the clinicians use, it's pretty spanky! I also have another brand new Wade saddle that I just bought. It is just as well built out of the same high quality materials. But, a saddle maker that didn't have the advertising power of a famous horseman built it. That saddle cost me $1650.00 and I got the breast collar and bucking rolls with it too, including shipping. The price has since gone up some but is still reasonable. I have another saddle that I've had for 20 years or so and it has served me well. I bought it for about $900.00 back then. But it wasn't *The* saddle I needed to fit in at a clinic I went to not long ago. So, I put the *in saddle* on my horse for the next two days just to fit in with the crowd. What a crock of hypocritical *bull$#it*!—and I went along with it! What you need to do is buy the best saddle you can afford that *fits* your horse, and your needs. That does not mean going down to "saddles-are-us" and getting the $99.00 special. A good saddle will cost you some money, maybe a lot more than you expected. But, if you save your pennies and get a high quality saddle and equipment to start with, it will last you a lifetime. Don't be swayed into thinking you just have to have this saddle or that just because everybody else has one. Or only saddles from this maker or that will work, cuz it just aint true and you'll wind up spending a lot more than you need to just to look the part! That's called bein' a "wannabe". A Wade saddle is a very good saddle for just about any general riding purpose. It will fit most horses and is comfortable to ride. But it's not the only saddle out there that will work, and getting one just to fit in with the crowd is a damn poor reason for getting a saddle that might not be the best one to put on your horses back.

I'm not even going to go down the road on what bit and bridle to buy.

Suffice it to say... *"If you know how to ride well, have good hands, and your horse knows what "whoa" means, then you can ride with a rope halter and lead".*

If not, look for something else to put on his head, train your horse better, or sell him. It's that simple. Personally, I'd prefer a horse that knows "whoa" rather than buying a bunch of crap, or trying to sell a barn sour racehorse.

Halters: Yes, I like rope halters with attached rope leads for the very purpose they were designed, as a training tool. They are strong, functional, and provide an extra bit of bite when you need to get a horse's attention. I have seen way more horses drag off their owners with a web halter on then a rope one. I re-enforce my horse's groundwork and manners on the lead every time I go out to get him so he never learns how to drag me off. A good rope halter helps me do that. You also can't leave a rope halter on in the field, unless you like going out one morning to find your $5000.00 colt hanging on the fence by your web halter, deader than a doornail. You also avoid those ugly halter dents in your horses' head.

If I go into a barn or a field, and the horses have halters on, it tells me one or two things…

Either that's a bad horse that can't be caught…

Or, the owner is too damn lazy to put on and take off a friken halter.

If the later is true, you're probably too friken lazy to take care of the rest of the things you should be doing as well.

Is that too cynical? Well, I told you this was a no bull$#it book and that's the way I see it.

Chapter Nine

Clinics—the Good, the Bad, and the Ugly

I have to take him to a clinic so he and I can learn more, fix this, etc., etc.

NO YOU DON'T!!!!!!!!!!!!!!!

And here's the reason why ...

You should have already bought a good horse that is trained to meet your needs. And, if you're riding regularly, haven't taught him any bad habits, and made a good choice in horses to start with, there should be nothing to fix!

I am not totally against clinics or saying we all can't learn from the professional horsemen and women who do them. But, if you are spending a ton of money going to clinics hoping to make a finished bridle horse out of your old racehorse, you're just plain nuts! Most people do not have the time or the commitment to do it, let alone the expertise. I've had horses my entire life, trained most of them myself, and they are very good horses. But, they are not bridle horses. They are good gentle horses that meet my needs and that's all I want. I can train a horse like that. I can't make a bridle horse and chances are you can't either.

If your having a problem with your horse and need some professional help to get it fixed, by all means get the help you need. This is not about being macho and getting yourself hurt doing something you can't handle. It's about enjoying your horse and not going broke in the process. Clinics can be a vary enjoyable and effective way of improving your horsemanship and spending more time riding. But, if you're going there and expecting some sort of miraculous change in your abilities or your horse in three days, you're there for the wrong reasons.

What I see at most clinics is a mixture of different horse people. Committed horsemen who are there to improve their skills in their chosen profession or passion, wannabe's (nuff said about them), weekend or casual horse owners/lovers (most of us), auditors and groupies. Yes, groupies. For the most part the ones who will truly get a real benefit from the clinic are the committed horsemen and women. They already have a lot of knowledge and know that if you don't continue the process when you leave on Sunday, it is not going to work by next Friday. For the rest of us, you'll get good information, have a good time, ride more than you have in a while, and that's about it, if you don't continue to learn and use it. As for the groupies and auditors, you can learn from that too. And, cheaper, I might add. About a quarter of every clinic's money generated comes from auditors. The people, who might not even own a horse but have an interest, or just want to meet the famous horseman or woman, buy a book or a halter etc. And some just want another notch in their buckle.

It's all good stuff. But don't be fooled into thinking that all your problems will be solved by going to every clinic out there and spending a bunch of money, because chances are, it won't for most people, just like buying every new fangled supplement on the market won't turn your 20 yr old gelding into Citation.

I'll may be ostracized by every clinician out there for saying this, but here goes. *Clinics are a money-making business for the people who do them, and if they weren't, the clinicians would be doing something else.* So if they need your money to continue to make a living, will they impart all their wisdom in three days, fix your horse (and you), so you can go out and conquer and not have to come back? I hear people all the time praising Allah for how much better their horse is after three days at a clinic, and yet they're at the very next one with the same problems. Why is that?

To be fair, in most cases it's not the fault of the clinician. He or she offered sound advice and helped you correct the problem. But what they don't tell you is, "If you had a good horse and you rode three straight days in a row at home and then regularly after that, you wouldn't have to pay me to fix it".

While we're on the subject of clinics and methods of training or the latest horsemanship phenomena, let me just say this…

If you are one of the people who place your trust and allegiance in just one trainer, clinician, or horseman, and follow him or her like a god or cult icon, then you're not ready to be a horseman and maybe not even a horse owner.

Why would I make such a statement? Because there is no one man or woman out there who has all the answers to every horses needs or problems, and knows how to fix everything. Or your problems either for that matter. And if you think that, then your missing a wealth of information out there that can help you improve yourself, your abilities, and make your horse better too. I'm not saying that you should jump from trainer to trainer every time the next new thing comes out. But take a look at what he's doing.

Maybe there is one little thing he does that's better than the other guy does. So incorporate that into what your doing, consistently… and see if it works better.

Too many times people go in the opposite direction and jump around from this method to that one because they saw it on, TV or read an article, or whatever. But they don't stay with it long enough and consistently enough to know if it works or not.

If you're going to change directions, at least give your horse a chance to get it.

That would be a good idea if you're riding him too. After all he didn't read the latest book!

What works for one horse, or maybe ten horses in row, won't work on number eleven. Then you have to find something else that will. Maybe your guru will be able to come up with something, maybe not. What then?

My best advise to you would be that going to clinics can be very educational and enlightening some times. But pick the clinic that best fits your needs and the needs of your horse.

Most people, (And I'm not Bul$#itting you here) should start out in very basic groundwork, horse handling, problem solving, or fear management, NOT HORSEMANSHIP! And God forbid, Not Colt Starting or Cow Working.

And to be honest, some of you should sit in on a basic horse care and knowledge class with your local 4H club!

I went to a horsemanship clinic not long ago and watched a young woman ride her horse around for three days. She was a pretty good rider and her horse appeared to be pretty well trained, even though she did mention the fact that she had come off him on a number of occasions. That aside, what truly amazed me was what happened when she was ready to leave, (even after spending three days with someone who could have helped); she could not get her horse to load in the trailer! She and a number of other people worked for hours on this horse and had little success. I left before they got him in, so I don't know how it ended. But it probably wasn't pretty.

Now why in the world would you go to a clinic to ride instead of a clinic designed to get that problem fixed first? I will say it again, clinics can be a very good way to get a problem with you or your horse fixed, but you need to do your homework and find the right clinic, horseman, book, trainer, or whatever, that will meet your needs.

My wife had a *babysitter* mare that we had to put down. I brought home another horse for her to try that didn't quite work out as I had planned…the wreck was pretty spectacular. After receiving my initial butt chewing and hearing in no uncertain terms, *that f@*$%!!!!*@ roan b@#ch will be dead* *or gone by morning*, I had to get her back up and riding *a safe horse*. Once she healed up, I did all I could to help her move past the fear of getting back on, but met with little success. So we had to find another way of going about it. What worked for her was to enter up in a horsemanship clinic that focused on fear management. The clinic was designed to deal with the rider's problems, NOT THE HORSE'S. Riding was part of this clinic, but not until the person was comfortable with the fear-management tools that had been taught and was ready to throw a leg over and ride. I'm happy to say that we are now riding together again and it's because we found the right help, not just the popular clinician or something that sounded fun to do. It was money well spent, unlike the money spent on a certain roan mare that will remain nameless!

Not all knowledge of horses, horsemanship, training, and life, (with or without a horse), can come from a single person—Including me.

Chapter Ten

Getting That Young Horse

AND BECOMING THE NEXT HORSE-TRAINING MOVIE STAR

Okay, I said I'd get to this chapter about getting a young horse, training, and your becoming the next famous horse whisperer, so now I guess we'll get to it. If you have really read this book, I mean *really* read it, you will have noticed that I've offered a few training tips here and there—tips that everyone should know and follow. But as I said in the beginning, this book is not about training your horse or teaching you how to do it. *I have also not made any statements about me being a professional horse trainer, marriage counselor, politician, movie star, or even an all-around good guy.* All I have tried to do is offer up some common sense logic and prospective from my point of view. You can take it for what it's worth, because my next meal does not depend on whether you believe me or not. So here it goes for good or bad, this is my advise to you.

All of you at one time or another will believe that you are ready or capable of getting that shiny new filly, raising her up, and training her just like the big guys. Then you'll take her out and show all your friends how great she is and just how you did it using all the latest videos, gadgets and what not. And you owe all this to the life changing experience you had at the colt-starting clinic you attended some time ago.

Maybe you're ready to take on the job of retraining that horse nicknamed "RBB" (pronounced Arby). That stands for "Rotten Bucking Bitch". (She's my horse, and it took a while to fix it because I didn't do it right the first time). And then, you too can go out and make your fortune in the horse world!

Some of you might very well be able to become a trainer.

Most of you won't, and are not, and will never be able to train your own horse or somebody else's!

I'm sorry to be the one who has to tell you that, but most of you will never have the experience, knowledge, commitment, or that little unexplainable but vitally important quality, or gift, that gives you the edge or the wisdom to become an experienced horseman and trainer.

In my experience, there are very, very few people out there whom I have met who I would consider as having that all-mystical gift, (according to some folks) of being truly able to communicate and understand horses. Being able to lay on the hands and calm the savage beast etc, etc, etc.

I have seen it mind you, and I believe that what I saw was truly a gift that I couldn't explain. But, I have seen it just once in my life and she is not old enough or wise and experienced enough to even know what she has! Someday I hope that she will realize that she is truly gifted and needs to continue to work with horses and learn from those experiences and teach others.

Sadly for all the young horses out there, most us will never have that gift and yet we'll go out and screw one or a lot of them up before we except the fact that we don't know what were doing.

I can and do start young horses. Not as a professional trainer or clinician, but as a person who has owned and worked with a lot of horses in my life. I learned my skills (as rudimentary as they may be), from many very good horsemen and women and some trial and error on my own. I've spent the time and effort it takes to be able to figure out how to work with a young horse or an older one on their level and ability to learn. I'm also not afraid to get help, if I need it.

This wasn't something that magically appeared or was bestowed on me just because I wanted it to happen, read some book, or watched a movie. I don't think it was some mythical gift I was born with either. It takes a lot of time and effort and a commitment to do something right, the right way. I have been called a perfectionist and been told that sometimes I spend too much time doing something that can be done half-assed and still pass muster. Well, that just might be something that's wrong with the world today. Everyone wants instant gratification, instant wealth, weight loss, or knowledge, but they are not willing to put in the work it takes to make that happen.

The finest trainers and clinicians in the country have spent their lives working with and learning about horses. That is how they reached the level of wisdom it takes to make a living at it. They weren't born with it.

You can learn to be a reasonably good, perhaps a very good horseman able to train your own horse, but it won't happen overnight. You will have to spend time ON a lot of horses and around a lot of horses. You will need to seek out all the knowledge you can about training. Books and videos might give you a start, but you had better plan on spending a lot of time around some good trainers perhaps mucking stalls, brushing horses, and saddling their colts for the opportunity to glean some of their knowledge. Remember that little old man at the stable who you think can't possibly offer you anything, or maybe that working student who may not have all the answers but has that special something with horses that we all wish we had.

When I worked at the boarding stable, I had 33 women in the barn and one man. He was 80-years old and had horses all his life. His Reining Horse Association Membership card was #39. We would talk often about horses, training, and just about everything else you could think of. Guys have a tendency to stick together when you're out-numbered. He was not famous, not well-known or rich, but he was rich in knowledge. I would watch him day after day try to give advise to some of the other boarders and see how frustrated he would get when they didn't  listen. Why? *Because they figured he wasn't up to speed with the latest fad in horsemanship or training. (And that's Bull$#it too)!* Well, let me tell you something. I learned more about horses from that man than from any video, magazine, or clinic I ever attended. One sad day at the barn while he was playing with one of his horses, (which he did most every day), he had a heart attack. I had to give him CPR. He didn't make it. I am glad he left this world doing what he loved to do, but I am sad that he took all that knowledge with him. I've learned some of what that man was trying to give us, but it's everyone's loss that we didn't take the time to learn more. What a pity. I miss him.

So if you get to the point of wanting to take on training a young horse, do what it takes to do it right. Then, and only then, should you go out and get that young horse and try to become a trainer. There are enough young horses out there now that have enough problems to keep good trainers busy for a long time to come. So don't go out and create more of them just to satisfy your ego.

As far as re-training that problem older horse goes... Well, the same holds true, but remember, now you're not working with a clean slate like a young horse. You're trying to change the habits of a wise old horse that has eaten and beaten would-be horse trainers like you before. So if you're feelin' Froggy just jump on!

And stick this book in your back pocket so it will cushion the blow to your dumb ass and give you something too read while you're healing up in the hospital.

That's about all the advice I can give to you folks on buying, and training a young horse. And if you decide to do it anyway, I wish you the best of luck, and you can tell me how it's going at your next clinic.

The key to making a good old horse out of a good young one is time in the saddle, not time in the stall.

Chapter Eleven

Parting Shots

This about concludes my ramblings about you and your horse. I could have made this book a lot longer by putting in a bunch of crap about my life experiences, childhood, or all the places I've been in the Coast Guard. Or I could have told you stories about a lama and chewing tobacco at a truck stop, (as funny as it is), and spent four years writing this… But, it probably wouldn't do you much good when that new colt you bought is up on his hind legs about to tap dance on your head, (and all you can think about is, I paid 10 grand for this?) now would it? So I hope that some of you will benefit from this book and say, "You know, he might have something there, and that I learned…" And I'm sure some of you will say, "Oh this is just another "Billy Beer" scheme to make money off the famous brother". And that's ok too. Because every famous person out there rode someone's coat tales to get where they are. So suffice it to say take this for what it's worth, and I hope that some of it will help you out. I know for me it has… Because for me it's been a very good distraction, (and something that I think needed to be said), to take my mind off the fact that:

Right now I'm laid off from work. There are still bills to be paid and I have a colt in the field that I should be working. I have a broken shoulder that I have to have surgery on before I can even think about getting another job or working my colt. And . . .

But tomorrow is another day, and hopefully I'll still be around to carry on and enjoy my horses and life, just like you. Maybe I'll get the chance to help you out with your horse, or just have a cold one and "*Bull$#it!!*" somewhere down the road.

And just for the record, I think most of my friends would tell you I'm a pretty good guy, too!

Think about this—I wrote this whole thing in about three weeks! Just imagine what you can do with your horse, (and yourself), if you put some time into it! I'm sure it'll come out better!

Thanks for listening to these whisperings!
Smokie

This little story has absolutely nothing to do with this book, but I thought it was pretty good, especially the moral!

Bagging Potatoes

Babs Miller was bagging some early potatoes for me. I noticed a small boy, delicate of bone and feature, ragged but clean, hungrily appraising a basket of freshly picked green peas.

I paid for my potatoes but was also drawn to the display of fresh green peas. (I am a pushover for creamed peas and new potatoes). Pondering the crisp fresh peas, I couldn't help overhearing the conversation between Mr. Miller and the ragged boy next to me.

"Hello Barry, how are you today?"

"H'lo, Mr. Miller. Fine, thank ya. Jus' admirin' them peas. Sure look good."

"They are good, Barry. How's your Ma?"

"Fine. Gittin' stronger alla' time."

"Good. Anything I can help you with?"

"No, Sir. Jus' admirin' them peas."

"Would you like to take some home?"

"No, Sir. Got nuthin' to pay for 'em with."

"Well, what have you to trade me for some of those there peas?"

"All I got's my prize marble here."

"Is that right? Let me see it."

"Here 'tis. She's a dandy."

"I can see that. Hmmmmm, only thing is this one is blue and I sort of go for red. Do you have a red one like this at home?"

"Not zackley. but almost."

"Tell you what. Take this sack of peas home with you and next trip this way let me look at that red marble."

"Sure will. Thanks Mr. Miller."

Mrs. Miller, who had been standing nearby, came over to help me. With a smile she said, "There are two other boys like him in our community, all three are in very poor circumstances. Jim just loves to bargain with them for peas, apples, tomatoes, or whatever. When they come back with their red marbles, and they always do, he decides he doesn't like red after all and he sends them home with a bag of produce for a green marble or an orange one, perhaps."

I left the stand smiling to myself, impressed with this man. A short time later I moved to Colorado but I never forgot the story of this man, the boys, and their bartering.

Several years went by, each more rapid that the previous one. Just recently I had occasion to visit some old friends in that Idaho community and while I was there learned that Mr. Miller had died. They were having his viewing that evening and knowing my friends wanted to go, I agreed to accompany them. Upon arrival at the mortuary we fell into line to meet the relatives of the deceased and to offer whatever words of comfort we could.

Ahead of us in line were three young men. One was in an army uniform and the other two wore nice haircuts, dark suits and white shirts ... all very professional looking. They approached Mrs. Miller, standing composed and smiling by her husband's casket. Each of the young men hugged her, kissed her on the cheek, spoke briefly with her and moved on to the casket.

Her misty light blue eyes followed them as, one by one, each young man stopped briefly and placed his own warm hand over the cold pale hand in the casket. Each left the mortuary awkwardly, wiping his eyes.

Our turn came to meet Mrs. Miller. I told her who I was and mentioned the story she had told me about the marbles. With her eyes glistening, she took my hand and led me to the casket.

"Those three young men who just left were the boys I told you about. They just told me how they appreciated the things Jim "traded" them. Now, at last, when Jim could not change his mind about color or size....they came to pay their debt.

We've never had a great deal of the wealth of this world," she confided, "but right now, Jim would consider himself the richest man in Idaho."

With loving gentleness she lifted the lifeless fingers of her deceased husband. Resting underneath were three exquisitely shined red marbles.

Moral: *We will not be remembered by our words, but by our kind deeds to others as we pass through this life . . . for life is not measured by the breaths we take, but by the moments that take our breath away.*

Author Unknown
(But someone I sure would like to learn from...)

About the Author

Smokie Brannaman grew up on a 5000-acre horse and cattle ranch in Southwestern Montana. Working with horses, cattle and rodeoing as a professional trick roper was his way of life as a youngster. Upon graduating from high school, Smokie chose to serve his country in the United State Coast Guard. Although his military duties did not always allow much time to spend with his horses, he never the less, rode and trained horses of his own and others throughout his military career. Smokie retired in 2000 from the Coast Guard and worked as a corporate operations manager for a security company. But he soon realized that his true enjoyment came from being around horses, training, riding and helping others with their horses. After working for two years as a stable manager for a large boarding stable, Smokie hired on at Ots Sunrise Farm to work with the young horses halter breaking, ground work and starting horses under saddle to progress to more advanced training. Smokie utilizes the training methods of his brother Buck Brannaman, Jeff Griffith, Clinton Anderson and others, as well as his own techniques learned during a lifetime of working with horses. Smokie lives in Greenleaf Wisconsin with his wife of 25 years, Susie and their three almost grown children, Kat, Travis and Jason. He raises and trains registered quarter horses of his own, which he uses as, Cavalry horses for his hobby, Civil War reenacting.